Sister Sorrow

poems by

Rachel Landrum Crumble

Finishing Line Press
Georgetown, Kentucky

Sister Sorrow

ACKNOWLEDGMENTS

Grateful acknowledgement is made to the following journals, in which these poems first appeared:

The Blue Ox Review: "Night Driving"; *Poetry Miscellany:* "She Dreamt of Fishes," "End of the Season, Change of Heart"; *The Louisville Review:* "Soliloquy of Anger," and "You Will Travel Far and Wide for Business and Pleasure"; *Calliope:* "Late Night Letter to No One"; *The Thorn:* "Winter Prayer," "In The Company of Poets," "Thinking Again of Job"; *Southern Poetry Review:* "Forgetting French"; *The Lee Review:* "Calling"; *Saint Katherine Review:* "It's Hard When All You've Got is Morning," "Metaphors for Her Suicide," "Against Responsibility," and an earlier version of "Meditations on Mortality"; *Stickman Review:* "Sister Sorrow" and "Hold the Moon," (which was also reprinted in *Rio Grande Review*); *Sanskrit:* "Composite of a Mother"; *Reed Magazine:* "Panic"; *Typishly:* "Protocol for Wings"; *The BeZine* "The Poor"; *Beyond Words:* "New"; *Last Leaves:* "Unclothed"; The anthology *Images of Heaven: Reflections on Glory* (Harold Shaw Publishers): "The Third Day" and "There and Now"; The anthology *Carrying the Branch: Poets in Search of Peace* (Glass Lyre Press): "Black Friday"

Special thanks to Chattanooga Writers Guild and members of our monthly poetry workshop since 2015: Helga Kidder (host), KB Ballentine, special friend Cynthia Young, Finn Bille, Karen Phillips, Chris Wood, Wes Simms, and to Diane Frank and the amazing constellation of writers in her online Poetry Workshops, including Mary Rummel, Claudia Reeder, Helga Kidder and KB Ballentine, where many poems in the last section of the book were born and sharpened.

Gratitude to Plug Poetry and the big-hearted Christian Collier and to Chattanooga Writers Guild Kate Koen Landers and Ray Zimmerman for their kindness with social media promotion, and to Claire Bateman, who has walked with me through doubt and sorrow. Thanks to Kelly Hainwright for her enthusiastic support.

Thanks to Tom Griffith and friends at Greater Formation for walking with me since the pandemic and for helping me get clearer about my purpose and design. Lastly, I want to thank my extended family, my childhood friends and neighbors from Deer Creek, Indiana, and my church family at New City Fellowship, Chattanooga for their love and support throughout my life, as well as with preorders.

Publisher: Leah Huete de Maines
Editor: Christen Kincaid
Cover Art: Erika Couey
Author Photo: Henry Christian Crumble
Cover Design: Rachel Landrum Crumble

Order online: www.finishinglinepress.com
also available on amazon.com

Author inquiries and mail orders:
Finishing Line Press
P. O. Box 1626
Georgetown, Kentucky 40324
U. S. A.

Table of Contents

To the love of my life, Jim Crumble, and our children Danielle,
Dallas, and Christian, to my best friend
Patty Caldwell Cunningham
who turn my mourning into dancing.
In memory Flora Miller Landrum,
and Dallas Davis Landrum,
who loved me well.

Part I. The House of Mourning

"The heart of the wise is in the house of mourning..."
—Ecclesiastes 7:4

Sister Sorrow

Perhaps it is the full moon shining high
above March rain clouds
or the quiet—like restored sanity—
reclaiming the house

or maybe it's the refrigerator's calm hum
like a grocery cash register, adding
digits of individual human suffering, unable
to reach a grand total, and the seething
narrowing eyes from the checkout line—

maybe it's the pure light of my daughter's
innocent dreams dividing the darkness
or the even breaths of my son
as he rides the purple dolphins of his dreams;
or maybe it's the methodical snoring of my
husband, determined even in sleep...

maybe it's my own pain that shimmers like wind-
chimes in the rising storm, the rising breath
of sorrow. But Sister Sorrow calls my name
from sleep, sets the table, lights a candle.

Aside from sleep, I had no plans, and, yes,
I can stay for supper.

A Story

The little girl is sad today. Her mother has left her body
in bed for days, has gone on a long treacherous journey in her head.
The child must not wake her, or the witch will come.
Her father leaves his anger, like muddy boots by the door.
She puts them on and runs outdoors to a thawed field.
The March mud sucks the boots up to her knees,
nearly swallowing her. She cannot lift her feet. It is dusk.

The windows of the house light up. No one calls her. Far away
her grandmother is praying. A storm is coming. The child must leave
the boots in the field and crawl on her hands and knees through the deep
cold mud to the edge of her yard. As she crawls, she sings,
"Take my small hungry body; make me a star or cloud. Let me float away."

The witch finds her. She has the green eyes of her mother, and her long
slender fingers. They cool her forehead; the girl closes her eyes
and pretends to feel safe. It is dusk. A storm is coming.
The windows of the house light up, but no one calls her.
Her grandmother is safe, but she is far away. The child sings
into the darkness: *"If I were a star or a cloud, I could be lifted out
of my small hungry body. I would be light and air. I would disappear."*

The witch tells the child her father is evil. The words drip like blood
from her pale chin. The girl wants the witch to take her to her mother.
The air turns cold; the little girl warms her hands in the faint glow
of her grandmother's prayers. The witch says: "I am frightened. Tell me a story.
Tuck me in bed. My mother never loved me. I was my father's favorite, but
he was never home." The little girl kisses the witch goodnight, and tucks
 her in the sandbox. Walking through the darkness to find her mother, she
enters the house of strange weather. A storm is coming. It is coming
through the windows; it is coming through the walls.

Composite of a Mother

In an imagined life, you conjure
a mother who sleeps nights instead of
pleading with God or wrestling with demons,
whose life has an ordered spontaneity,
like rows of cedars in the winding French countryside.

For each child, she orders cross-stitched
birth announcements, instead of personalized
astrological charts. She reads, paints,
works at some quiet
sensible job: an office manager, a curator,
a midwife, instead of living borrowed lives
as a minister's mistress, a gangster's
girlfriend, a model, awaiting the next
trust fund check to pay the rent
on the red-shingled bungalow
in the second-hand suburbs
on the outskirts of affluence.

She can give without bankrupting herself,
take without bankrupting you.
She enters your life by the front door;
she doesn't sleep on the back porch
of your sorrow, coat stuffed with rejected
manuscripts against the night cold.

She flies in, years later, to see
the grandkids, helps make Thanksgiving
dinner, is lighthearted, takes her place but not
your heart. When it's time to go, kisses everyone
goodbye, leaves small gifts and funny notes
under pillows like the Tooth Fairy.

She doesn't steal out the window of your life
like a thief at midnight, taking only valuables,
leaving behind the chaos of anger, the cut
glass of grief, the small change of regret.
You search yourself for that mother,
but cannot find her, an amateur
       detective, with so few clues.

Aftermath

for my mother, and for Sharon

Reading about hairless laboratory mice
started it, making you dream of nothing
but an angry red ball in white space, coming closer,
closer, until it was large as the world.

That's when you took up painting,
as if you could mute the glaring edge
of need, as if with your watercolor wash
you could forgive God for everything.

If you had taken up quilting,
the fabric of your Grandma's Sunday dress,
the linen tablecloth you ruined as a child,
your father's silk and acetate ties
would configure to become something whole,
but not wholly good, wordless, but not
without speech, like any good comforter.

You merely want to fix the broken.
Somewhere there is sanity to such propositions.
Somewhere, you think, those pink-skinned bodies
scamper from beneath ultra-violet lights,
put on fine fur coats.

Bones

Cold cement bruised my bones
as I balanced on my stomach and flat chest.
Rocking like a hobby horse,
back arched, my small arms strained
to grasp thin ankles.

Madame, who once danced with someone famous
on a far-off stage, sat on a cushioned mat,
made us feel endangered.
Years had thickened her muscular thighs.

Down a long corridor of years came the singing:
"...Come, soothing death, come sweet repose.
Bear me away in gladness."

My sister, carrying a nest of bones in her body,
said she had remembered those grand plies
and feared they'd bend my soft bones to breaking.
Now her child, nearly seven, is as old as the news
of my mother's fall.

Instead of calling, my proper grandfather mailed the news
my sophomore year in a stoic carbon copy letter,
sending me up five flights of anger.
In a bus, up 81, the landscape drained
of all color. And I learned from my mother
to carry my body like a breakable thing.

Outside Charlottesville Hospital, or long
before, going home from ballet
I must've stepped on a crack—
at least twice. But I don't look down.

I wake, after dreaming all night of wheelchairs:
place my feet on the cold floor,
make my bed, and walk.

This Curtain of Morning

for my mother

I walk in leaf-littered air.
Handfuls of birds dot the sky,
like peppercorns thrown against
the sheer curtain of morning.

Why then, do I imagine your death at all?
Sunlight angles in, cutting
patterns on green-brown lawns, thinning branches,
shop roofs, hubcaps. Your hands

grip the scarred metal
of your chair as you wheel
through San Diego's static green
October. My thoughts lean
towards you as trees here
lean South against the wind.
Remember how you mothered me
out of your hurt, how I mothered you
into mine?

Summer nights when you'd wake us
to the moon's rising over vast dark
fields, winter nights when the voice
of your prayers snatched me from my sleep?

My heart heals slower
than childhood wounds did, stinging
in ocean water. I want you to know—

not the inevitable anger, but the healing
that comes, slow as seasons, that as I walk,
takes me by surprise.

Houdini

"...and unto the Lord Jehovah
belongeth the escapes from death."
—Psalms 68:20

I.
She's done it again, that great Houdini
tried it on for size
like some evening jacket, glamorous
in the department store mirror,
gaudy in the light of day; she's
called it back to her
like a stray cat who'll come only
at supper time.

How many lives does anyone have,
each time, nearly landing on her feet?

Like Houdini in the water tank
behind the curtain
her job is not entertainment, but
survival—she survives for a living.

II.
Mom, what sleight of hand could
take you out
of your body, anchored
to the metal frame of your chair?

What act of God could make you
live in that body
broken and whole,
freed from the violence
of your own hand?

The Third Day

That November morning, we chased whirling leaves,
laughing.
   She walked in forever Spring.
We caught autumn in our lungs, our warm breaths
gathering with clouds of birds blown South.
     She brightened
 with effortless song, clear as Craig Pond in August.

When the phone rang, we splintered, silent and separate:
my son to his baby dreams, my daughter to the long shadows
of a season turned cold, me, to the frightening slow-
motion tremors from the Pacific Coast, rocking my kitchen
floor through fiber optics.

 She became one with that water,
    diving into the perfect
 circle of the sun: whole, as if never
 broken, standing inexplicably up,
 when constellations rise to sing
 the Hallelujah Chorus.

The topaz and garnet leaves we'd gathered
to cheer her flat green San Diego autumn
wither, unmailed on the mantel.

 At the morgue, her spent body lies cold and tagged
 three days empty.

Metaphors for Her Suicide

I cannot leave
flowers, cannot go
to her grave, 600 miles
away, at least.
Do not want now to
embroider her pain, enough
is enough.
Want only to find
my own way in the dark—
transform the unspeakable
into words. I wouldn't
let myself see how
she was constantly
giving things away:
table linens in a shoebox,
the scrapbook: pictures, drawings, sayings,
all sent the month she
made her will. She divested herself
of this world—a light bird
who could fly to heaven.

Yet rehearsals couldn't ready us.
She forced God's hand
like a fist
through a plate glass
window. She got through, all right,
but left behind
such fragmented
light.

Against Responsibility

Soon the rain will stop; sun will shine on steamy streets.
Watch: already blueberries on the bush are pink
expectation, the white moon, a hand mirror in the blue depths.
Why couldn't I matter more to her than her pain?

The world is sweet; we are born to bitterness.
The sun on skates glints down the mountain.
The soil lets go its damp breath. Spring blossoms, long
spent, give way to fecundity.

Soon this season, too, will be spent. But now
a bright bubble of calm floats across the pasture.
A fly pirouettes above my head. Constellations run their courses.
The sun on skates glints down the mountain; we pull off the road
to study the map. We have lost our way.

At the Writers' Conference

I am the girl at the 7th grade dance, wilted
flower on hunched shoulder,
                    shoulder against the wall.
This moment is too important to matter.
If I close my eyes, it will be over
                        so I can long for it.
But to be here now, in my grown-up polyester
blouse and midi-skirt is excruciating.
                                I stare
at the row of black polished shoes, shifting
tapping to Donnie Osmond imitating Michael Jackson
                            singing
"One Bad Apple Don't Spoil the Whole Bunch Girl,"
ready to give up on love.
                        Two shoes walk past mine.
My steady hasn't talked to me in the two weeks since
we exchanged ID bracelets through a friend; we've never
                spoken at all. By the punch bowl,
my best friend Patty is laughing hysterically at nothing.
Two shoes echo across the room,
                            taking hours to reach me.
We share loneliness on the dance floor,
too shy to speak or let go; then I speak
                            and he lets go.
Now I am couple number one. I close my eyes and move
to the music that's played twenty years in my head.

If the room is not bathed in this particular
melancholy, which, like love, makes everything too
important to voice,
                    then don't tell me, don't
tell me, don't tell me.

Years Later

for Jim

The abusers travel 700 miles to retire down the street.
They wear the kind faces of your aging parents. They say
they did not move to be near you. They seldom call
and never visit; they simply don't want to impose.
They've had time to think, and they think your punishment
incomplete. Their familiar anger surfaces if you visit too much
or not enough. They have worked hard. They have the things
they want; somehow you were not one of them.

They remember you as irresponsible, accident-prone.
you remember your father's rage powering you
through a window, how your allowance bought a new one.
You have tried to be the perfect son, and for this
they are civil, dutiful, almost gentle.

You are tired of scavenging the wreckage of your childhood.
The fuselage offers no shelter, the black box, no answers.
Your wife is calling you to supper.
Your children watch with longing
through the window.
You want so much to come home.

Urban Living

The landlord's nephew died
last month. I had to move out.
Their grief could not be contained.
The walls began to bulge, plaster cracked
even before I heard the news.
One man got stuck in the corridor,
had to be pried loose.
The Yannessas tearfully apologized,
said it was no use:
Grief had come to stay.

After the tenants move out of the fifth floor,
complaining of constricted
space, the bank will repossess the building. Nights,
only the thinnest derelicts will sleep there.
And later, when it is condemned and torn down,
grief will live on in the rubble,
not knowing the difference.

song of the garbage man

for Marliss Kapitz

i see the city from the back
of a truck—histories within each plastic bag,
and i'm talking *garbage* day, not recycle day.

each bag shamelessly set out, from the curbs of
row houses in west philly, to the wrought iron
gates and well controlled lawns of mt.airy and
society hill. little of this could be salvaged: snagged

nylons, spent condoms, rotting leftovers, broken
big wheels, well-worn shoes, wilted roses. this is real,
not pretty, but not a lie. we live out lives whose
evidence is verified only by the things we

throw away. i threw away my life once.
I ended up searching for it at the landfill
but was overwhelmed by the teeming congregation
of rife garbage, would-be yard sale treasures,
obsolete files.

instead i found a place
where appearances don't deceive, where rejection is final,
where secrets are exposed to the searchlight of the sun,
displaced gulls, impassive weather.

so i became what i am: america's keeper of secrets,
scribe of sorrows, transporting
not disembodied economic theories
as i once did in the classroom, but the stench

of mortality, full-bodied grief,
the refuse of the city's bright
promise: not veneer, but substance.

this is the life i chose, finding no other.

The Poor

In the sky, it's raining backwards,
always backwards. From where we stand,
it is a nightmare— our tears are the sprinkler system
of heaven. The clouds grow lush and green.
They tantalize beyond our ability
to desire. We stand, poor,
with sand in our shoes, and
dust in our mouths, holding buckets
upside down to catch the rain.

Part II. The Hell of Chaos

"I prefer conquered to conquering countries.
I prefer having some reservations.
I prefer the hell of chaos to the hell of order.
I prefer Grimm's fairy tales to the newspapers' front
pages."

—Wislawa Szymborska "Possibilities"
Nothing Twice, Selected Poems

End of the Season, Change of Heart

Rain sifts through grids
of grey cloud, telephone
wire. The lopped branches
of badly pruned oaks ache
in the bracing air.

There is nothing here
I do not know by heart—
how the "white trash" old mother
and daughter with their idiot
look of intermarriage

will continue to push the baby
in the stroller
as they have for three years;
nothing changes but the baby,
now an idiot child

cannot walk. A tall pimple-faced boy
grown derelict
still wanders these streets, face frozen
in a surly grin he hasn't
the sense to unsmile.

Evenings, I watch for clouds
of birds. They are returning South from
that river in Daniels, the abandoned mill town
just below the Mason-Dixon, where I swam
my fifteenth summer.

I move about the house recalling:
four o'clock tea at my grandmother's,
off-season weekends at the shore.

The mongoloid called
Owl Man rides his banana seat
bike, playing his rusty harmonica
all over town. And wait—
I see him stop

for two black women who lovingly
clap and dance in a circle,
bowing from their thick waists
as he plays.

The wind calls through the door.
It sings with the voice of the sea:
"Orphan of time, orphan of time,
all your safe harbors are gone."

Fire Sale

See how the banana moon sinks in Venus'
unblinking eye, and let go that anger-
colored balloon of grief. Watch it rise in this night
sky like a negative sun
whose light years out-distance
death's slow dark yawn.

When the balloon's string is no longer
tight around your finger you will forget
as a child forgets a kiss given late at night
which enters her dreams as a breeze on her cheek.
In the morning, she is unmarked, yet
bears some vague comfort into the day.

Something on the radio
suggests that dream you almost
remember: "Due to smoke damage,
everything must go."

Tonight I Hang Clothes on the Line in the Almost Dark

The moon shines imperfect, opaque above the scrub pine.
Locusts shimmer like tambourines in the night woods,
filling the air until there is no room
for silence.

At 25, I found I was the same age as Barbie, and somehow
that made me older than I thought—older than my oldest
sister, who dated guys like Ken
who came to the door and shook hands with my father.

I never dated a guy who shook hands with my father,
so it's hard to believe I'm no longer 25, and no longer the devoted
understudy of my sister's teenage life.

The neighbor lady calls her five dogs one at a time,
her shrill voice rising above the shimmering moon,
my husband's opaque dreams.

And now I learn, too late, that the night owls,
those solemn narrators of my childhood, have startled off,
were really mourning doves.

You Will Travel Far and Wide for Business and Pleasure

You will dance on turquoise seas.
Sharks will only nip at your heels.

You will sleep in the safe hammock of air.
No one will cut you loose.

You will study German in Tibet
and ask no questions.

You will enjoy fame for paying taxes
and putting out the trash.

You will sprout green thumbs
from your two left feet.

You will lead a life of wanton
asceticism, followed by tidal winds.

You will receive the Nobel Prize
for your obscurity.

You will meet your hurricane of desire,
and beach many stars.

Forgetting French

Martine, I never wrote you because I feared
the grammar of my thoughts would not fit
the grammar of words, particularly yours,
the infrequent language of my dreams.

In Tours, English escaped me, but *la langue* was as vivid
as the flowers in the stalls on market day
near La Place Plumereau, as palpable as the steam
rising from morning bowls of café au lait
on my way to the *Institut*.

I'm not the American friend you'd hoped for.
I started a letter to you from *la gare*
while waiting for the all night train from
Paris to Amsterdam, but a north wind blew
right through my summer clothes, sent
the aerogramme tumbling down the corridor.
I hadn't the strength to find the words again.

In Amsterdam, merchants spoke to me in Dutch
and something soft as cotton wool
settled in my inner ear, separating me
from the rhythm *des paroles*.

Sometimes those syllables beat in my sleep,
insistent as the liquor-breathed sailor who
knocked all night at the door of my cheap hotel
room in Perigeux. In the morning, they are gone,
leaving only a trace of something not
unlike fear, or joy. How do I get back?

Now, six years later, I shut the blinds against
the autumn darkness and your word *tenebres*
falls from my tongue like a still-green leaf.

The Traveler

Gradually, you
become a foreigner
to your own body.
Your body no longer
resembles you. It
keeps appointments you
did not make. Children,
grandchildren come
with Minoltas and cassettes
to authenticate
your existence. They want you
to tell, retell how
your Quaker mother was baptized,
turned out of Meeting, how
your father invented a gauge
that measures the thickness of steel.
They are timid birds,
nibbling for whatever
winter-blasted berries
can be gleaned.
Inside, it is Spring;
you are the same self
you've always been—
trying to speak French
in that port city dress shop
in the forties;
only Hindustani comes out.
Always, the steamer trunk grows
heavy with travel.

> *In memory of Margaret Haines*
> *and Isabelle Miller*

It's Hard When All You've Got Is Morning

Night lets you off at the corner of Sleep and Six-thirty.
The alarm blasts like the horn of a car
careening past as you step off the curb of comfort
onto the cold wood floor.

It's hard to put your body back on, to collect one's
self as one might gather a stack of
scattered papers, hard to march one's self
out into the traffic of morning when morning
advances against one like an angry mob of urgencies.

It's hard not to see the fog caught
in the trees as a heavy shroud, and gravity,
not as a safeguard against floating
through space, but as a wrestler's
grip, forcing one to one's knees.

It's hard when all one has is this moment—
no, this one—and what can't be seen
is the sun, burning through the curtain of cloud
until the opacity, though luminous vapor,
is no more solid than a sigh.

It's hard when no hint of a golden afternoon
or a flame-blue sky hangs over the highway
on the crowded commute to Usefulness and Industry.

When Purcell's *Trumpet Voluntaire* rings out
over the car radio, who could guess the light would
grasp the shroud of fog at the corners,
shake it into a gentle rain? Who could believe
that urgent angry mob would so easily dismiss itself
in an orderly fashion? You never know.
You just begin again.

She Dreamt of Fishes

for Bonnie and Joan

She dreamt of fishes last night;
grunions flapping their silversides
on Pacific Beach, four days past
high tide. Terrible
moon-bodies rose up
on buried tails, gave back light.
their brightness made her eyelids
twitch. She

dreamt of fishes last night while
sperm swam the dark
womb of her sleeping
daughter, 900 miles away.

It is always like this.
She rises, thoughts gathering
like weather or wind,
that black line on the sea's horizon.

Her daughter wakes, less ephemeral,
late, tired from late love,
her husband's scent draping her
bright body. She slips on a gray wool
suit, leaves the house
smelling of soap.

Her mother will call tomorrow, her small voice
bobbing, buoy-like above the static
of distant connections to say she's pried
the bronze from baby shoes.

Reality Realty: A Gallery of Homes

I. *Suicide. Her Apartment: Chula Vista, California November 1990*

In the house, all was order and absence. She made
her last accounting. Notes in drawers about who she wanted
to have what. Six photocopies of a handwritten will, updated twice.
All the pictures of her six grown children placed
face down before her last terrible act, as if they wouldn't see.
No letter. An empty teacup on the table. The sons are hushed
and worshipful, the daughters, irreverent, numb with grief.

II. *Depression. Daughter's home: Chattanooga, Tennessee 1989*

In the house, all is chaos and clutter.
Crushed Cheerios, unfolded laundry, toys, litter the stained
carpet. Important papers and wedding photos are lost in the attic.
The house is small; every room is lived in. In warm weather, they must
spill over into the backyard.
The people are light and airy, intense
and brooding. The house fills up with indecision.

III. *Abuse. A Classmate's Home: Abington, Pennsylvania 1971*

In the house, polished curios sit on dusted shelves.
Clear plastic vinyl runners access the white sitting room
to no one. In the next room, cruelty is served precisely
at 8 a.m. with poached eggs and English muffins.
Full attire is required. The perfect guest never arrives.
Only the people are cluttered and dirty.

IV. *Schizophrenia. At Home: Deer Creek, Indiana 1960-69*

In the house, all was whispered fear, anger on tiptoe—
the mother was sleeping—or a frenzied cacophony of laughter,
pea-shooter battles, slamming doors. The stuffed clowns
rode child-size rockers, chariot-style, down the hall
cheerfully pulling dolls by shoestring nooses in their awful
wake. The father was silent, the mother sick—both somehow
absent. The children huddled together, or ran for cover
into their own bruised, forgiven futures.

Early Autumn: A Long Ago September

I.
Sitting at your kitchen table
in a Southern city
you wonder where it is you want
to get back to, when the green odor
of dying leaves gives itself up
to late August rain.

In this fading light, your worn clogs
remind you of the early rustic paintings
of Van Gogh. In Amsterdam, at the museum, you cried
to see that precision unhinge in broad
textured swirls, like pain.

II.
This is the place you find again, where fall
has surprised you, in your layers of summer clothes,
sandals and socks. Bells from Dam Square send off
a flock of school children on bicycles,
braids and leather book bags flapping.

The air is strangely thicker here,
heavy with the smell of fried potatoes and beer.
They speak a language your blood
understands. You shake your blond head
and over a table of antique rubber stamps,
place two gilders in large expressive hands.

III.
At your desk, you cover the blotter with the stamp's
image: sailboat on a rough sea. Was it you,
or another, discussing God in French
with a Moroccan at the hostel, along an alley
where sequined ladies solicit from their
doorsteps in the tall shadows of late afternoon?

You see how the shadow of this other

flickers, like lamplight.
You watch her cross the Zuider Zee
under the low grey ceiling of Van Eyck
and follow the blond bearded Danes North—
The road home is always North.

Six Most Important Things:

1.
Buy a Collie and name her Magritte. One warm January day,
she will leave a single, bloodless
bird's wing on the porch step and trot off
into your childhood.

2.
Do lunch with Barbie. Let her go on about her Dream
House, her pink Ferrari, life with Ken. Then compare
scars; you're "one up" every time. Ignore
her plastic smile. Ponder the possibilities
of breast augmentation.

4.
Take a spin in your dream ego's powerful red
convertible. Get lost in the traffic of the Rose Parade.
Smile. Wave. Scan the sky for clouds.

4.
Pick up your boots at the shoe repair. Volunteer
to teach a self-help group at the Community Center
on how to pull yourself up by your bootstraps
while walking backward into the Aegean Sea.

5.
Send entropy a sympathy card. Years later,
you will find it in a pile of unopened mail
in the attic.

6.
Let your mind become a pressure-cooker of impressions.
Lift the lid and the steam will burn your face
and disappear.

First, fold the laundry.

Calling

Ridges bristled with winter dead trees
lift the highway beneath my tires.

The alarm clock, the quiet of the house at 5 a.m.,
the bills on the kitchen table are calling.

7 a.m. twilight: up interstate 75,
my headlights are part of a moving
macramé of light.

The wind in the trees, the telemarketers,
my fourteen year old's adolescent loneliness is calling...

Unseen currents tear a ragged swatch
in the grey cloud blanket,
exposing astounding blue.

My friend whose marriage is crumbling,
ungraded papers, panicked students are calling. Above
the din, my 5 year old's simple request: "Mommy, play with me" is

Calling: dirty laundry, my mother's absence,
my daughter's fledging bright future is calling.

My husband's sonorous laughter, unwritten stories,
an uncertain future: calling...

Partly sunny? Partly cloudy?
Same old question.

World sadness is calling. A still small voice is calling.

My cell phone is ringing a minuet.

Without voicemail, or
caller ID, the heart
is forced to pick up
or hear the incessant ringing.
How else to know it is not
The Call
we've been waiting for?

Part III. Creation, Working Itself Out

"Mission: to be where I am.
Even in that ridiculous, deadly serious
role—I am the place
where creation is working itself out."
　　　—Tomas Tranströmer *"THE OUTPOST"*
　　　tr. Robin Fulton

No Sleep

because the fire in the woodstove
lapped my dreams to ashes,
which trash men collected, along with rotting
leftovers, at daybreak.

I had wanted to turn on the sun like a search light
To find out why my neighbor always cries past midnight,
to silence darkness, yapping in the woods.

I had wanted to put my ear to the fallow garden
to hear the heart of the world which beats like an aging
Somali child's.

Instead, I popped a donut in the microwave,
warmed some milk while Cambodians crawled to the border
on their hands and knees through the endless Kampuchean jungle,

While bones rotted in mass graves in Serbia,
and the offspring of the dead, spoils of war, slept
in the houses of military commanders
dreaming of nothing, forgetting their names.

I want to raise my consciousness like a flag
to mourn with those who mourn, weep with those who weep,
but I'm just too damn tired.

I wish I could slip on my sunglasses and back
into the womb, where light is opaque, has no blunt edges,
but the sun rises like a search light,
and it's too late for sleep.

Soliloquy of Anger

I am the Housewife of the world.
I shine my samovar, I watch for sales
on Chinese milk, Egyptian beans;
my family dines by candlelight.

There's nothing tamed
I can't make wild.
I make ferocious love each night
and rise to bare the breast
to screaming, greedy child.

Anger, my mother's diamond
brooch, catches light; it goes
with everything.
Survivor, like my Swedish
Ivy, Wandering Jew.

Late at night, when I've clipped and
saved the coupons, words unsaid
buzz, trapped houseflies
above my aching head.

Soil under my fingernails. My garden
of sweet and bitter herbs, stoic in this
lunar light. Shadow of the tamarisk.

Sudden glass cut
in my calloused summer heel
and I never dreamed the blood so red,
so real, staining the flagstones
to the kitchen door.

Angerama

Let's trade angers, like baseball cards. No, let's
hunt for more at yard sales, till we have a matched set.

No, let's vacuum, dust, sweep, mop, straighten
and polish it so we can invite passivity over for dinner.
Then Passive and Aggressive can hold bitingly polite
conversation. Let's study its composition, sharpen our technique

Learn at the feet of the masters, so we can have a showing
at a gallery, invite all our friends. Let's alter its genetic code,

X-ray it, recommend arthroscopic surgery to strengthen its
knees. Let's teach it to dance: the electric slide, or
ballet: graceful, effortless on steel-enforced point.

No, let's truss, baste, slow-roast, fricassee, flambé it.
Let's feed on it for days, like Thanksgiving turkey: anger

chili, anger fajitas, sweet and sour anger. Let's make good
use of it, cooking even the bones down for soup.

Thinking, Again, of Job

As the bombs fell again
in Aleppo and Raqqa, I stood
in my classroom talking about fragments—
how to make them whole—and felt the frightening
absurdity of pressing on with fixing
comma splices, stopping run-ons, while the world
runs headlong over an abyss, like the swarm of swine
Jesus commanded the legion to enter.

This world knocks the words out of me, like a
sudden fall, flat to the earth winds a child, who
because of pain cannot cry out. My work, then, is to be here
listening in silence, like one of Job's comforters—
comforting, at least, until the first foolish word
crosses the mouth's threshold. But I pile them like stones
so I can stand on something of my own making, claim
perspective, a kind of singing in the dark: the voice a luminous
beam in an amorphous fearful country, a way of asserting
I am here in the face of overwhelming evidence

otherwise. This is not about you; it's about falling down
in a fallen world and falling asleep in a dark room
instead of singing and waking up in the half-light
surprised to find sixteen years since my mother's fall,
two falls since her death, I survived. Though I have cursed
God, I did not die. And though she died by her own hand,
her life is not a fist for me to shake in the face of God.

But what is it now? A cipher, a remembered lullaby
sung to my children at bedtime, a travel bag of old letters,
a moonstone ring in a halo of sapphires with one stone
                    missing...

Domestic Injuries

Hours after our words opened old wounds
we hadn't meant
to remember, anger is the amphetamine
which shakes me awake, jump-starting
my brain when my body can't move.

How can I reach you with your silence—
that tough, brittle carapace
around your heart?

I wish I was Jacob, thigh out of joint
from wrestling the angel. Instead, I'm
Rachel with a baby wrestling in my belly.
I fear you'll shut me out like my father, or
abandon me to illness like my mother.
All I see ahead are sun spots, hot and angry.

Rehearsing losses even in sleep, I had this dream:
you are hit by a car on some mission of rescue.
You suffer from internal injuries, and I awake unable
to fathom a world without you. How
many injuries do we sustain, how many
unspoken between us?

Stretching my ligaments, knocking
against my ribcage, crowding my heart:
this need for you grows daily within me.

Daylight falls like sleet against the window.
Love, I cannot give you something perfect
as a dark bird's flight
even on this miserable morning.

Keeping Up

for Jim

Love, I've run through the heat of June
with your easy stride beside me.
Now along this gravel trail, our steps
are muted by September's first leaves.
Can we go the distance?

Your mind is like a map,
pointing you to your body's
farthest boundaries. Darkness
nips at our heels. Your pace quickens,
but I falter.
You press toward
a foreign country I fear I cannot enter—
impenetrable as the silences
you keep. Though I try to keep up,

my mind loiters by the river's hard surface,
watching how a shard of web catches
a grey leaf motionless below a rain dark alder,
keeping one moment from the next.
Only our bodies stir the air.

I wish I could tell you:
It hurts to love you.
Come, run your finger across my pain.
Let me swim in your Ethiopian eyes.

But what I cannot say presses in on me
like this darkness at our backs.
If we spoke now, the clouds of our voices
would rise like prayers and dissolve
with the last light.

Separation Anxiety

I. Mother
You I left sooner than I wanted.
You could not hear me, but the voices,
the voices that made you separate
from yourself—no home for even you
to come home to. Now you live alone
and who can help?

II. Father
When you left last month, I was ten
again, grieving the loss of you
in my daily life. Last Christmas
when you fell suddenly asleep,
open-mouthed on the couch,
I feared a world
without you.

III. Husband
In bed at night, a slower rift
of pure fatigue distances us.
I do not welcome your touch, only
the kiss of sleep, then hearing your
even breaths, I'm wide awake, reproached.

IV. Daughter
When I go to work, you tell me:
"I will cry for you, Mommy." I joke
that I will cry for me, too, aware
of your subtle manipulation,
innocent aspirations to make it
without me.

V. Son
Now that you can crawl, you fear
your ability to leave me, mine
to vanish around the corner,
out the door: that power of leaving
bonds us.

Late Night Letter to No One

I have come to this place of quiet
where the dogs howl at nothing,
where the crickets fall silent
after midnight, and I am tired.
Tired of the meaningless artillery of syllables
like rain on a trailer roof.

Give me birds' song before any other music—
the faraway drone of a car on the blacktop,
the steady interrogative of the night owl
rather than the muted dialogue from a late
night movie through the screen door.

In a cluttered desk, I save friends' letters,
but write few, timid as I am
of my own incessant loneliness for words.

Always, in my mind, I say all I have to say,
write reams, fill the hungry mouths of others.

Silence, a voice from the darkened hall of my childhood,
whispers my name. A scared child in a dark room,
I defy the silence and sing.

I send this out, as Noah's dove; first to find evidence
of solid ground, then to release it to that unknown place.

Winter Prayer

There's a heartbeat in my belly
like a runaway locomotive through a train trestle—
all fierce motion and distance.
All day trees bared black arms against a winter white sky.
And all day I have seen the world
as a passenger in a car—the particular
blurs insignificant; only where I'm going matters.

You offer perspective, but I want answers
that rise like heat from the oven
of my cold kitchen. Yet you came
as helpless, as determined
as this heartbeat in my belly.

There is nothing I can offer
but the voice of my prayer,
small cloud, which rises and dissolves
in this December night's air.

Part IV. From Mud Puddles to the Beach

"God, like any good father… drags his kids kicking and screaming, from their cherished mud puddles, to take them to the beach."

—Andree Seu, from *World Magazine* "Messy in the Middle"

New

for Danielle

Birds small as butterflies call river-breeze
through alder, its bleached leaves rattling
like old grief.
They sing this February day
to Spring and almost I believe
Spring only a song away.

For seasons my body has labored toward ripening;
this year it ripens toward labor.
All that was green has bled into the river
which ribbons through these woods
like a jade dream of summer.
This small one kicks at my touch
the way wind follows water.

Tiny roots clutch the afternoon-thawed earth;
so much possibility!
A marching band plays in the distance—
a real one. Sunlight scours the air.
How differently I view the world.

Anniversary Poem

for Jim

I.

My mind is a white sheet flapping the wind.
You are the clothes line. No—a reflecting pool,
your thoughts of me, bright goldfish. Without them,
you tell me, the pool is empty, stagnant.

I would rather be a hawk flying so free that I
see you, a hand mirror of the blue heavens. Spiraling
closer, I spy luminous fish, murky depths beyond
the pond's hard veneer. I break the surface, talons
out, grab your first bright thought, fly off to safety
to feed on it. You are troubled. New thoughts spawn
under the shadows of clouds, below the wind.

In winter, I sail those currents to warmer climates
dreaming the pond liquid as summer. From the sky,
you look like an unblinking grey eye. Your bright thoughts
swim sluggish, surreal beneath opaque ice. I wait for spring.

II.

Love, this game is old. Let's play a new one:
You are earth. I am sky.
I rain and shine down upon you.
I draw from your waters to fill my clouds.
You are solid ground beneath me
I help you grow; you hold me up.
We are not afraid to need each other.
On moonless nights, it is so dark,
                    we touch.

So Few Confidantes

for Dallas James

Morning comes like a white moth with wet wings
clinging to the screen door (its only horizon)
unable to let go and fly.

I awake, heavier than my body,
grieving again. A man in Amsterdam
is dying in the faint light of my prayers.
So. I cannot stop the rain to pick blueberries,
cannot heal or comfort him.

My son strokes the moth's wet wings, studies
its iridescence, asking," Why are your tears?
Are they for my white grandma?"

Last week, he put his head on my shoulder,
said into my eyes, when another plan was
thwarted, "Calm down, Mommy, calm down.
In a few minutes, God will tell you the secret."

But God, you have so many secrets
          and so few confidantes.

Brévent

All distance and muted sound. A vast
blank feeling of
insignificance on that snowy peak
opposite Le Mont Blanc—called Brévent.
Watching, from the cable car
when the fog thinned, a child sledding
so small, from this perspective
she could fit in my hand.
I hear that distant
roar. Unseen cataracts
beyond undecipherable
white of too-bright snow
and fog—or the furious
deafening roar
of silence?
           The fog now
lifted, the child and her father
still there and I marvel
at the father's faith
that she would not go over the edge,
not be swallowed by oblivion
next time fog obscures.
Then, see as if in a vision—
or an airbrushed postcard—
the surreal peak of
Le Mont Blanc against a sky so
blue, only faith
could conjure it. In the valley,
suddenly tangible
and present: a hang-glider.
Spiraling slowly up, up...
I want him to light on that peak.

I want to be him,
to be his eyes looking over
the aurora of the heart
        of the whole world.

Hold the Moon

I.
Wading through the cold current of your silence,
                     I am waist deep, going deeper as I move
towards you. Your skin of night is soft and hot
                     almost against me, but an ice floe breaks loose,
pushes me away. For a moment, I forget to breathe:
                     the cold air, dangerous, jagged in my chest.

What a pair we are: you fear intimacy; I fear abandonment.

Love, think of the continents
our blood has traveled to bring us here.

II.
You are a house without doors; I am a house without walls.
It is raining. Open the window and let me in.

III.
Does my unrequited love for words render you silent,
or does your silence render my love for words unrequited?
All I know is when the words come, in my torrent of loneliness
you are left looking silly, helpless as any man
desperately clutching an umbrella under a volcano.

IV.
Six years ago, I lifted our daughter high
                     under a December night's sky, until her small heart filled up
with words of longing:
                 "Oh hold you moon."
Wordless lexicons opened up inside me. And I felt held in that moment.
(Is this your language, and will you teach me?)

                 Never mind, love, don't
speak; just hold me like that.

A History of Desire

I. Baby Teeth

Already, I am nostalgic for her mouth, innocent
of them, dread the interruption
of her mouth's sweet suction. Last night, all twenty
bloomed in my sleep—glittering utensils
needed to digest the world.

II. The Body

Desire: candy for the eyes.
How sweet, how frightening to be that
candy in the mouth of another.
I remember being eleven or twelve when desire grew
like the puzzle of downy hair between my legs,
small breasts rounding with secret ripening. I was
walking with my sister by a Maritime Academy
in Castine, Maine when the ivy-covered buildings released
their dangerous charges and suddenly I was seen, not
as a child, but as a dizzying object of desire.
I thought it some mistake that they should call and
echo the tumult in my blood, that the body
which I'd comfortably inhabited
now inhabited me.

III. The Heart

On a plane, my body aches after two weeks
of no touch, and a man in a black business suit keeps
looking back, the same ache in his eyes.
I am home. Tires hit the runway and I can't wait
to be held in the arms of my children,
and my husband, to be both object and subject,
again to be one.

Waiting at the Urologist's: A Letter to My Mother
Eight Floors Up and Six Years Late

Even from the examining table, sheet across my lap, waiting
I watch the variable weather from 8 floors up. I conjure
pictures in the clouds: George Washington, a dog, the fearsome face
of an angel. Sea billows, and then I remember early autumn weekends
in Atlantic or Ocean City. I guess September's sudden turn away
from summer drew no crowds, so hotel rooms were cheaper.

Does being given a life no one would choose make it cheaper?
When did the insidious self-loathing start, or was it always crouched and waiting?
A North wind cut through Meshed, Iran to your nursery window, snatched away
your happily-ever-after. Now, 70 years later, grey storm clouds conjure
the passing off-season of your life. We loved those stormy weekends.
The turbulence of ocean and sky was like your, our, pain we could not face,

could not deny. The strange peace of abandoned beaches, of your lovely face
blown calm. The few opened Boardwalk shops offered summer clothes for cheaper
than the winter clothes we'd need. We wanted nothing on those weekends
but the moment, suspended dangerously, like the gulls we watched, waiting
between two seasons: wings outstretched, aloft whatever storm winds conjure.
I watched you spend that joy, pocketing a few small coins before it passed away.

Once, you stood on the dryer in your nightgown. For a moment, God looked away.
Your arms flung wide, like the crucified, a deluded Messiah we could not face.
Who nailed you there, suspended in grey filtered light? We could not conjure
what god you cried to, but your mother's prayers held us all, not some cheap
beloved affirmation you taped to the wall: "Divine Order." You, waiting
for some kind power to seize your mind on those long manic weekends.

Now I see how frightened you were, wrestling that fallen angel alone, weekends
when a train or bus carried Becky and me to the surreal safety of our father, away
from you. We didn't know how scared we were, trying to believe you, waiting
to see who would meet us again, the witch or the fairy godmother? Which face
was yours? Both or neither? Your life was precious to us. You thought it cheaper.
Schizophrenia was your abusive lover, our cruel stepfather. We couldn't conjure

his name. I've spent my life trying to save you, to save myself, us all, to conjure
a cure: lifeboats to stay afloat in your chaotic weather, those weekends

off-season. You tried so hard to stay afloat, to drown, thinking yourself cheaper
for your pain. Now I know we misunderstood you, now that you've gone away.
I did more than I could; you know that now. I thought I couldn't bear to face
a world without you. How long has this Urologist kept me waiting?

It is my own life I now must conjure. Alone and waiting
one weekend, I took back the self that goes on without you. My face
bears your likeness no cheaper. Here, mostly clothed and in my right mind,
I'm waiting.

Past Imperfect

for my father

I knew she was flawed. But you I needed
to be perfect, and so you were:
perfect as Orion in the night sky—
glittering, distant, steady enough to navigate by.

Your light, not so much warmth as hope,
and alone in the dark it was sometimes
enough. I knew you were busy
in the universe of responsibility

and I tried so hard not to want more.
I saw your sadness, and yes, your shining
constellation of anger and tried not to be
the reason, tried to fit myself into the smallest
possible space

and not breathe. I thought
that's the only way I'd be allowed to stay
under your safe canopy.
Now I see I shouldn't have
been so good I disappeared, which is why
it took me so long to matter.

Duck Pond at Abington Friends School

As I walk this gravel road near Georgia
I think of that place, in a safe
suburb of Philadelphia, ten years forgotten.
Perhaps because the "V" cut in this pond's still surface
heals to the banks, and on, to the pasture. The white

mare reminds me of the silver-haired Headmaster,
shy and gentle in his important blue blazer.
Birds twitter like children in the Meeting House
stillness. You break the silence of that hour
by standing to sing "How Great Thou Art" while I
stare, humiliated, into my adolescent hands.

Mom, I always thought you sang from an exquisite,
self-inflicted sorrow, the kind I could not bear.
Today, I break from my own self-conscious silence.
Raising a woman's voice towards the mallard's flight,
I sing with all my strength a song I've never heard.

Departures

It is March. I am flying away from Vermont's
mud season, imagining the dogwoods blossoming
in Tennessee. The landscape changes
imperceptibly. Sculpted brown earth rises
from a variegated patchwork of plains,
forming winding ridges like the grey folds
of the mind. News of my aunt's death fell
from a cold night sky with the last snow of winter.

Now, four years and four months from the day my
mother took her life, I touch grief's wound, surprised
to find a sealed scar instead. I hear her voice, still
but only from a great distance.
How is loss understood? One must guess
at dimension, distance flattening out
mile after rolling mile.

So this must be the neat geography
of forgetting: Variations on winter-
dead fields becoming those almost
green with early spring. The silver veins
of creeks following grey rivers.
Pencil thin warm currents etching
a lake's frozen surface, until its slow
pressure weakens deep walls of ice,
which groan and let go into the clear
unblinking green eyes of ponds
further south. But who thinks of snow

in the mountains when drinking cold water
on an summer afternoon, or even now
of people wearing parkas in Chicago
while the Tennessee River glints below me
and the pilot announces a balmy 82 degrees?

I once believed: The road home is always
North. Now landing amidst a lush
and gentle southern Spring, I leave behind
the winter-dead to bury their own.

There and Now

Beauty finds new voice there. Not this heart-
breaking elegy of ululating song.
Here, where late summer leaves turn dead
green, there the painter dabs a touch of yellow
so that Spring becomes a way of life. There, too,

Regret turns like an arrow in mid-flight,
becomes joy exploding brilliant as fireworks
in the never-ending day.

Here, imperfection marks the trail to beauty,
just as sin, a night sky, shows the brilliance
of grace, a full moon.

There that moon is but one in a galaxy of bright
planets, the first letter in a mysterious alphabet
whose lexicons cannot exhaust words of praise.

I prayed with my mother on the phone
days before her death. Later, in a dream
we prattled like school chums
on the alpine peaks of Heaven, her now
violet eyes washed of their green envy.

The prayers of my ancestors
echo peace to me across the canyon
of eternity. When I am destitute of history,
of hope, I have only to lay down my head
and listen.

Night Driving

It's amazing what a body can do when pressed,
when the road is nothing
but the converging beams of my headlights,
when all but the Hayden symphony
shining like the digits of my car radio
is lost to the fog.

I can feel my body, heavy as fog
being pressed to oblivion by sleep's deeper
gravity. Headlights letting go
of darkness, giving way to the music of lights.

No. My hands grip the wheel. I am
real. The eighty-second symphony
lifts the car above mountain roads.
I am pressed to intuit
the turns, to think with my body.

Later, I'll say it was nothing
but the static taking over
the concert on Public Radio,
how the sonorous voice of the concert master
became an ellipsis—amber reflectors
along the yellow line—

How when the audience rose in applause
in some concert hall in Minneapolis,
I was miles above the valley,
and gaining altitude.

For Spring

*Fantastic to feel how my poem grows
while I myself shrink.
It grows, it takes my place.
It pushes me aside.
The poem is ready.*
                    —Tomas Tranströmer

Skin becomes dust to pare us down to the essential,
even as we live. Death, too, is a process.
In the April air, green worms let themselves down by invisible
silk cords. My eyes are the yard, looking
up at the sun. Birds carry motes off, find them useful.
Go, sing to this mute world songs of beauty.

It is hard to imagine untainted beauty
without suffering, which has always seemed so essential.
The neighbor children find our rotten apples useful.
They smash them when they fall from the bough, a process
of giving way to swallowed anger. When no one is looking,
they throw the brown imperfect fruit hard. They throw them down.

After, I sweep the pulp and apple skins off the drive, down
to where skins become earth, nourish things of beauty.
This year, daffodils bloom when no one's looking.
My anger is dust; only the lilacs are essential.
I dig up layers of leaves and birds' bones in process.
Seeds settle in, set down roots, make death useful.

The earth is so forgiving to find this failing useful.
It wears death like a light shawl, a comforter of down.
trees stretch awake, yawn green in this season of process.
Light fractures light, scatters beauty
everywhere. We are amnesiacs, remembering everything unessential,
like the dove whose wing beats touch my head, who stands looking

to make sure I'm not there. My eyes are the yard looking
up at the sun. Birds carry motes off, find them useful
for a nest. What remains is somehow essential.
Jays swim the air, diving, not falling, down.
Go, make of my failure things of beauty.

A Dream in Which You Are Walking Again, And the World is Whole

It will be a day like this: the first of Spring.
Large islands of clouds will float across the heavens
blue as a flame. Only a hint of storm overhead.

The alder will confetti the air with dry brown leaves
which have clung like old grief all winter.
My neighbor will wake from cancer as from sleep,
or death. I will swim the sky to you.

You will be running along Pacific Beach
singing a sweet, unwounded song.
Daffodils will nod their heads in the breeze.

It will be a day so beautiful, it could break your heart.
But your heart will never break again.

Part V. Wonder

"Did I say that the only thing we require to be good philosophers is the faculty of wonder? If I did not, I say it now…"

—Jostein Gaarder *Sophie's World*

An Apologetic of Flight

A defiance of gravity,
a spit in the eye
of physical probability.
A Six Flags for the soul,
a way to match flesh and spirit,
step for wing, finite with infinite.

As a child, flying was a dormant power
unleashed only in sleep.
And sleep was an escape
from the world of impossible gravity.
And gravity was an inscrutable calculus
to solve without so much as the wooden abacus
locked in my father's study.

There were boundaries I was made
to break through— but in my waking life,
I was afraid of heights, and the door closed
against the darkness
of my mother's bedroom, and the Witch
when she rose up
in the body of the Fairy Godmother.

That's why I have been training
since childhood for flight,
as if my spirit flew
before I grew roots, was earthbound,
before being knit together
in my mother's womb,
or anchored to her pain.

In my dreams, I had only to bend my elbows
to rocket straight up, or hover a foot off the ground,
a helium-filled balloon
on a string, wrapped around God's finger.

I will be recalled someday.
On windy days, the reflected light is blinding!
Meanwhile, since each day's cloudscape
is ravishing and singular, I want to rush to be one
with all that I praise, to fathom
the membrane between me and the world.

Child's Play at Deer Creek

We ice-skated in winter, swam in summer,
despite the leeches on the moss-slippery banks.
May-apples grew green parasols
in the cool of the woods in Spring.
We jumped rows of soybeans,
shredding our skin running through rows of corn
in summer, those frightening games of tag.
Barns of rooms we designed with stacked hay bales,
fields of tall grass trampled into mazes.

The smell of bubbling tar on an Indiana summer day,
shimmering blacktop, burning through our flip flops.
Blackberries stolen over the fence of an old maid's
overgrown field. Mulberries' seedy sweet sour mash
on our tongues, and underfoot, staining our Keds.
Nectar sucked from purple clover.

I had three recurrent dreams:
A red ball in white space came closer,
closer, until it was large as the world.
Sometimes it was a spider, or
a giant, like the one from Jack and the Bean Stalk,
shaking the earth. I fled alone
to the church basement
as plaster cracked. If I ran and jumped
just right, I could
catch a wind current and fly.

Patty's concrete porch became our stage.
With a jump rope for a microphone, we took turns
making up songs, full of unspeakable sadness
and loss we didn't know we carried.

When we were 12, too old for child's play,
we'd walk a mile and take our show
on the gravel road at sunset,
passing corn fields, long lanes leading
to family farms with silos,

a snaking stream, silver-pink in the last light,
returning by the light of fireflies.

Our voices were crowded out of our houses:
no room in my ranch-style manse by the church,
not in her rented white clapboard
two story farmhouse—every square inch
suffocating with our mothers' mental illness.
How did we know to cling to song
under a wide Indiana sunset,
when so little else made sense?

A Way of Seeing

"Look at your feet. You are standing in the sky."
—Diane Ackerman

When I was five, I found a parallel universe
under my feet. By looking down
into a hand-mirror and stepping high
through doorways,
I could walk on the ceiling all over the house.
Natural as nightly dreams of flight,
it fed a hunger that gravity would not have the final
word. *God, how I needed that.*

I then imagined my escape to College,
which I renamed Mortuary.
I pictured ivy-covered red brick buildings,
and a singular life of my own.
The school colors were pink and gray,
like evening clouds. I was a cheerleader.

My mother stayed in bed for days, weeks,
sometimes rising, clothed in Apocalypse,
pronouncing judgment
like an Old Testament prophet.
Sometimes when she woke, her illness fell off,
like Lazarus' grave clothes.
That's how I knew to hope.
Both hope and disappointment frightened me.
In those moments she was not
the shattered lamp, but the light inside.
She would dress, and make herself
up, and I believed her, every time.

She read us *1001 Arabian Nights*
when she was well.
Inspired, I snuck into my father's study,
put on his glasses
strolled the Persian rug and unlocked a world
of Byzantine Geometry undulating beneath my feet—

another triumph over the order of things.
Unlike Scheherazade, I told the listening universe
stories to spare my mother's life
for one more day.

Of Navigation and Memory

Flora Miller Landrum 1928-1990

The day you took your life,
alone in your Chula Vista apartment
you turned each of our pictures face down
so we wouldn't see.
Twenty-five years ago yesterday,
I was driving across Olgiati Bridge.
Lost in the grey folds of the mind,
suddenly, I knew before I knew, and
I could only weep.

As a child I used to dream I had to drive
the station wagon on some mission
of rescue in the dark,
no glasses, just the way I had to navigate
daily life with your schizophrenia.

Today, I sit by the window—
quiet November rain and intermittent birdsong
through 20,000 days of living under clouds
and sunshine, lost in the grey folds of the mind.

I see the towering fir, someone's Christmas tree
planted 35 years ago, casting our front steps in shadow,
the dark and yellowing needles of each branch
weighed down with memory.

When we meet again as contemporaries,
your six children will know you at last
in beauty without heartbreak.
We will browse our days as if each
were a tome on the shelves of a magical library,
each page a permeable membrane.

My brother says we have been honed
by the chisel of your life—

moving through space and time,
lost in the grey folds of the mind—
yet in the chiasmic wake of our loss,
the peace that eluded
you, the peace you prayed for your children
falls, mercifully, deliberate and nourishing
as the November rains.

Isthmus to Eternity

> *"For the gate is narrow and the way is hard that leads to life, and those who find it are few."*
> —Matthew 7:14 ESV

I.
Nearing 88 now, my father closes his eyes
to pull words through decades of storied
memory, encountering detour after detour
caused by Parkinson's, by his strokes,
so that if he can navigate at all,
the thought arrives in rush hour
stop and go traffic, two hours late.

Mostly, he persists
in threading memory's splayed filament
through the narrow eye of the Story
because *he must*—
the stories must be told; who are we
without our stories?

Orphans, mute patients wheeled down
antiseptic hospital hallways by strangers.
The test results may come
to tell us of our inevitable end,
but not the miracle of the journey.

II.
Emerging from the underworld of sleep,
my father must say goodbye again
to able-bodied-ness, to verbal fluency.
By his bed, the dogs are barking—
all he can say is "kids."

He must carry this body all day,
moving in limited No Time. Is it
slow as a season change, or like a treadmill
set too fast, always a step from falling?

My father's road to Golgotha, not unlike
the journey of all humanity, happens
in the maddening sprawl of 5 o'clock traffic.
It is cold. The windows are rolled up—a kind of
urban loneliness. Eventually one
gets to where one is going.

You Walked Me Half Way Home

We were the same age
in earth years,
but now you've passed me up
almost without notice:
the way a traveler,
beginning her journey, takes no
notice of the first mile marker
on the highway. But now
there are three of you in one car,
a big old boat of a Cadillac
with leather seats and a sunroof,
miles ahead of me, on this
endless road.

I want to say it's dark, and you light up
the night with your laughter,
singing along with the radio—
Motown Music: *Stop in the name
of love, before you break my heart,*
but your hearts
are diamonds now.

Becky, I'm earning the wiry grey hairs
you won in a windfall after
chemo took your long brown
crown of glory at 42.
My baby you cared for,
until you had no strength, is 17.
Your youngest is a mama now.
Your grave finally has a street
address. I visit often.

Ortestine, you taught me how
not to dance like a white girl,
not to stuff my anger,
and to dismiss trifling with:
"Honey, please!" I hear your
voice singing: *Going forth*

and weeping, bearing precious seed,
when it's time for harvest,
He shall come again! on an old
choir CD, and remember
the single tear that leaked
down your comatose cheek
at the hospital when I came
to ask forgiveness, and say
good bye.

Bambi, your name, like your life,
was a storm system. Heart breaking
that an East Coast ice storm grounded my flight
from Nashville to see you,
but you, determined as ever,
took flight from your Baltimore
hospice room, despite
capricious March weather, and,
as your last practical joke, Spring dawned
mild and clear the next day.

Haines, you ride a few miles behind
the rest, in a Prius Hybrid, no music
but the muffled snowfall kissing
your windshield.
For you only, there is snow,
because you clothed yourself
in solitude.

Near the end,
your family guarded you like
the Queen's jewels, and
we, your cousins were hired help
who might steal you away.
Allowed no other contact,
I conversed with you in poetry,
our native tongue. The bleak beauty
of your poetry and paintings haunts me now.

May my words be like hot coffee
at a midnight rest stop
along your way.

Panic

The trick is to look just
beyond the farthest point
of reference, the way
you did on family trips to ward off
car sickness: look straight
ahead, eye on a fixed
point above the horizon. Fixed,
but you are not, you are
moving, moving through time and
distance at an astounding rate.

And so, just like a dancer turns,
spots, turns, head snapping, eyes
fixing—for a moment—on one unmoving
object, so you, too, must find
dynamic balance, a way of tricking
your equilibrium, as if you
were now both the real and
the plastic ballerina of your
sister's jewelry box, toe shoes
riveted through with a metal rod
to the source of motion beneath
the red velvet floor.

Just so, you must remember
you are married to movement
no matter how nostalgic for stasis
you become: this is a vow
made before God and many witnesses.

And so you wake each morning with
Otherness in your bed and you must
remember the choices you've made
as you look in the bathroom mirror
and brush your teeth. This is the one
whom you complete with your methodical
vigilance. This is the one who completes
you with velocity and risk.

There is nothing to do but hang on,
a child on a carnival ride, dizzily
clinging to the safety rail, no time to
process now, hearing the scream from your
gut come out as a shout
of laughter.

Luminous

"The tipping earth, the swarming stars..."
—Kenneth Rexroth

I swim the darkness of my yard,
curtained by woods. I am searching for the ethereal
Sanskrit of fireflies above the tipping earth.
Nowhere, not even a pin-hole of light
in the growing dark.

Suddenly, in the towering scrub pines
the swarming stars flicker and blink.
They light the world from inside out.
From the scrub pines, soundless drum beat pulses
bright unfettered male imperative.
From the grass, females glow in uncertain
recognition: predator, or mate?
Some species call in rhythm,
some in syncopation.

Flash patterns, delectable as pheromones ...
I remember when we first met—
you from the tribe of synchrony, me from
scattershot—how your light called to mine
in the darkness. You didn't know:
I was trying to scare off predators.
Has it been decades, days, or hours?
Remembering lifts my heart again
sometimes in sync with yours,
sometimes in scattershot—
always in wonder.

While You Slept

for Christian

          the dreams
of the diligent evaporated with the first
light.
      While alarm clocks sounded
and coffee brewed, those evaporated

dreams, ascending as universal prayer
reached the stratosphere, congregated

in cumulous, then rained their
glory hallelujahs, joining crystal with

crystal and floated through
the atmosphere, a grey sky

touching the earth. Water became
iron. A stippled sky let go

the sudden scatter. Friends' texts
woke you from your sleep:

SNOW DAY! NO SCHOOL!

Meditations on Mortality

I.
It hurts right where
I do not now, nor ever will
have wings.

The residual pain that clamped down—
was it my heart?—
radiated over my collarbone
to my neck, left shoulder
to my elbow.

Driving myself to the emergency room
thinking, both, "This is nothing," and
"This could be it."

II.
2:30 a.m. Outside the ER in dirty snow.
An apparition of summer
under a street light: a tree full of gray leaves.
I yank one off, just to be sure of what I see.
It has the brittle flexibility of a carapace.
Perhaps the tree holds on
like the old woman in our neighborhood
who stayed in the house all week with her
dead husband during the snow storm, calling
no one, not even her daughter, then shot herself,
letting go for both of them.

Everything You Love Will Leave You

Your olive-skinned, green-eyed mother
whom you were desperate to save finally flails
out of reach your thirtieth year. You could not
picture her growing old for a reason.

Your father marries a woman 27 years his junior,
moves from the East Coast to Northern California,
too far to be with him when his final days come.

Your first born, aqueous and golden, makes you
an accomplice in her escape to L.A. at 18, and later marries
a man who only has eyes for Alaska.

Your middle child flies to New York City
like a moth to a flame—many holidays consumed
in his absence. Once his wings have brushed you,
iridescence is everywhere.

Your youngest, 17, rehearses his litany of leaving
with friends on weekends, longing for Denver
or any far-flung life his siblings forsook him for.

Your burnished bronze husband, tall and smooth,
will one day stoop and shuffle through the house.
His sonorous laughter, the muffled voices from the TV
will one day be replaced
with silence. Even your own
face in the mirror smudges and shadows
with the weight of years.

Go outside—the winter new moon
slung like a hammock in the black sky
above the mountain reminds you:
Everything you love was born inside a star.

Black Friday

after Emily Dickinson's "There's a certain Slant of light"

I. "There's a certain Slant of light"
Late afternoon sun squints
through the west windows.
I am content with leftovers and quiet,
my male child accounted for, and sleeping—
safely home.

II. "Heavenly Hurt, it gives us—"
A distant dog barks without conviction.
Traffic swishes steadily two blocks away.
The last of the gold and scarlet leaves
tumble from the trees.
Protesters in Chicago carry this message
down the Magnificent Mile :
"Justice is the public face of love."
16 shots and Laquan McDonald's
17 year old life folded like a knife.

III. "None may teach it—Any—"
A ladybug crawls across the screen, unfolds wings,
flies off. My synapses still smarting
from the 2 a.m. phone call …
felony charge, detention hearing…
Two weeks ago, I told my son, "Be careful
who you get in a car with.
It could cost your very life."

IV. "When it comes, the Landscape listens—"
Today, in Chicago, Paris, and Chattanooga,
shadows held their breath, mourning senseless violence.
Seven shootings in three days in my city alone.
The youngest to die in the Paris attacks was 17.
My son is just that age today.
I exhale. These are reasons why
the heart is convalescent.

Unclothed

This is what it's like to crawl, wet and gangly,
out of a cocoon—
not like finally peeling out of too-tight jeans,
but like scraping the very skin raw,
chapped and burning in winter wind—
numb and tingling, so that cold
alone could coax warmth back in,
preventing
frost's deadening bite.

Where are my old familiar clothes—
why now are they denied me?
What cruel joke is this
that I am thus exposed?
Change comes in hiccups,
no spoon of sugar can stop or sweeten.

A hopeful convalescent,
I wrap myself in poetry, sip hot milky tea,
try to equilibrate.

All day I have been quieted
by the hush and stutter of wings.

Protocol for Wings

Don't let their newfound weight
sink your shoulders
or snake your spine.
Pinch your shoulder blades together,
flatten your back, center
inside a feathered frame.

Don't be ashamed—only
the ones who were meant to
will notice. The rest will look
through you, as always, seeing only
their own need. Brush them gently
with your wings and they will remember
something halcyon and gone,
pushing past you.

Once, you, too, sleepwalked
through your life: Forgive them.
As for flying, practice standing tall,
for now, wings fully spread,
like a weight lifter holding a stance.
More instructions to follow.

A User's Guide for Chaos

I.
Begin the day with measured order.
As velocity increases, order will remain
like water in a pail
swung swiftly in a circle,
keeping everything at arms' length.
Warning: contact with moving or
stationary objects will cause order
to spill everywhere.
So much for centrifugal force.

II.
To prevent dyspepsia, take chaos only
in small doses
on an empty stomach.
If dystopia occurs, control is contraindicated,
the construct of fools. Seek immediate
beauty, silence, humility, and rest.

III.
If order is a wall, chaos is a claw hammer,
useful for demolition.
Choose targets judiciously.
Revolution requires revelation.
Objects like Time will outlast you.
Rage against it, and you will be pinned,
hammered by an invisible hand.
Accept the blows.
They are part of your humanity.

IV.
If "foolish consistency is the hobgoblin
of little minds," chaos is a window
smashed open in a locked room,
allowing exit. Do not fear it. Your future
will be illuminated, but only
as you crawl out the window,
one flailing foothold at a time.

Grief Reunion

I. *Ishnomaki Community Center, Japan.*
July 2014.
In the tatami room, the mourners'
faces are fixed smiling masks.
Their eyes are not smiling.
The Tsunami of Sorrow
has taken whole villages out
to sea. It spewed back
rubble, and a few broken
bodies. And now we are
here together with each of our
losses, packed inside,
like Russian dolls, our layered grief.

II. *Stillness*
Blue white winter morning
one day past Christmas.
Fog lifts from the valley.
Pale blue sky slowly
grows deeper than eyes.

III. *Root Chakra*
Wedge of glass in the foot
sudden shock of blood.
Root of bitterness in the heart
rising taste of death.

If I feel the earth
firmly beneath me on this mat
I may weep for brokenness,
or joy that I am held up,
that I will not collapse under this weight
of sorrow. The yoga instructor says,
 "See yourself arriving here."
Why? I came but took no notice, mind going
in many directions…oh:
When my father died, I was miles away.
Because I did not arrive, I cannot leave.

Later, my voice carries across an ocean
to translate this epiphany for my daughter:
When I die, be with me if you can.
Hold me, so you can let me go.
The earth will not hold me up forever.

IV. *Fear Has Many Names*
and my body knows them all—
the heart pounding for no reason
at midnight in the quiet of the house,
rehearsing for catastrophe.
The tightening in the hips,
hamstrings and knees that makes
my footfall heavy on the stairs, the clamping
neck and shoulder pain that closes
my heart, shortens my breath, the churning
stomach at the sumptuous feast.

If anger is a fist, sorrow
is a limp hand.

I want to dance in the pelting rain,
arms overhead, holding nothing,
sing while the water
flows down my face,
into my open mouth.

I want Jesus to walk that treacherous tableau,
command me out of the peril
of the boat onto the strange safety
of the waves—
if only I don't look down,
if only I don't
look down.

Again

We parted, stoic characters in a 1940's wartime movie—
Grief, waving a white hanky on the pier.
It took hours in the blinding heat
for the steamer to finally pull away.

I, a helpless spectator on deck,
counted hankies until I was dizzy.
Who doesn't suffer loss?

Eventually, I saw the world—the Alps,
Venice, the Pyramids. That long ago farewell
no more than a dark line on the sea's horizon.

Months into the journey,
on a flawless blue day
I spotted Grief waiting at the pier
in a gray fedora and trench coat
as we neared a foreign port of call—Malta, or Haifa.
Something not unlike love
leapt in my heart.

I thought "good-byes" your forte,
didn't expect to meet again
so far from where I started
on an ordinary lovely day.

Rachel Landrum Crumble's collection *Sister Sorrow* spans decades including decoding childhood with a schizophrenic mother, depression and the grief of losing her to suicide, negotiating all stages of adulthood, marriage and motherhood as a white woman married to a black man living and raising biracial children in the South.

She received an MFA from Vermont College where she studied with Leslie Ullman, Mark Doty, and Jack Myers. She received scholarships to Bread Loaf Writer's Conference out of grad school and later to Vermont Studio Center. The majority of this collection was edited in a Post Graduate Poetry Manuscript Workshop at Vermont College with the late Jack Myers. She has read her work and been interviewed on WUTC, a local NPR station with Richard Winham.

She taught first at an inner city preschool and kindergarten, then as an adjunct at Covenant College, UT Chattanooga, Chattanooga State, and was Director of Developmental Writing at Cleveland State Community College. Later, she taught high school English at inner city schools in Chattanooga and was a Visiting Lecturer in English at Lee University before working as a Resource English and Inclusion teacher in high school in rural Northwest Georgia. She and her jazz-drummer husband of 40 years live in Chattanooga, TN. They have an adult daughter and two adult sons and just became grandparents in 2021. She has two other poetry manuscripts ready to edit, and fiction projects to continue. Look her up at poetteachermom.com